CHURCH SCHOOLS

A Guide for Governors

GEOFFREY DUNCAN AND DAVID W LANKSHEAR

The National Society (Church of England)
for Promoting Religious Education

ISBN 0 901819 44 1

Printed by The Good News Press Limited, Ongar (01277) 362106

Preface

In 1984 the National Society published a discussion paper about the role of the Anglican Church in education and particularly Anglican schools. This publication, *A Future in Partnership,* marked the beginning of a process which has led to greater clarity about the role of Anglican schools. This new booklet is a further part of that continuing process. It supersedes two previous booklets – *The Church School* (1990) and *Governing Church Schools* (1992) and provides an introduction to the workings of Church schools for governors, teachers and parents. It can only be a starting point for further reading and experience, and governors and teachers will find that there are a number of National Society publications particularly designed to help them in their tasks. Some of these are listed at the back of this booklet.

Governors of Church of England and Church in Wales voluntary schools have to discuss and make decisions about a wide range of activities and policies. Many will be similar to those with which the governors of any school have to deal, but some will be appropriate only in a Church school. The aim of this booklet is to help governors by providing outline guidance and preliminary advice about their responsibilities. No two schools are the same, so it is not possible to give precise guidelines which will work in exactly the same way for every school. Indeed, there are three different types of Church voluntary school: aided, special agreement and controlled, as well as Church grant-maintained schools. Throughout the booklet, where the law is different for the different types of voluntary school, this is indicated.

The booklet follows the same order of subjects as the Department for Education Booklet: *School Governors: A Guide to the Law* and is designed to be used in conjunction with it.

Since it is not possible to cover every event in a school or each matter of concern to governors in a publication of this length, they will need to know about other sources of help and advice. The principal source of guidance, other than the Local Education Authority (LEA) and the Department for Education and Employment (DfEE) is the Diocesan Board of Education (DBE); the Diocesan Director of Education can always give help or advice which is specific to Church schools.

Contents

Note: Governors are also recommended to study the following National Society publications (see page 40):

The Curriculum: A Christian View

Religious Education

School Worship (collective worship)

Looking for Quality in a Church School (Mission Statements and inspection)

Church School Staffing

What Makes a Church School Distinctive and Different?

1 Even in the last century this question was being asked sufficiently often for one leading cleric to place his answer on the record. Archdeacon Denison confidently asserted that "'Church school' means only a school into which no child is admitted unless baptised or being prepared for baptism." Few Anglicans today would advocate such a rigorist rationale for Church of England or Church in Wales schools, and even in the nineteenth century many people disagreed with Denison.

Governors of a Church school today should spend time reflecting on what makes their school different from (not necessarily better than) a county school. Their answer will affect every area of policy in their school. If in practice their school is not in some way distinctive and different, the question must arise – why have Church schools?

The Church's recent responses to the question "Why have Church schools?" have frequently drawn on the green paper published by the National Society in 1984, *A Future in Partnership*. In this the author suggested ten characteristics which, in varying degrees and proportions, should mark a good Church school. A good Church school is:

(i)   A safe place where there is no ideological pressure and yet Christian inferences are built into the ethos and teaching as signals for children to detect.

(ii) An ecumenical nursery which builds from children's fundamental unity a sensitivity to difference, and the faiths of others.

(iii) A place of distinctive excellence which is not just tied to what is academic but plainly linked to all aspects of the life of the school including the manual, technical, aesthetic and non-verbal.

(iv) Stepping-stones to and from the community, for children, staff, parents and local interests. The school learns to be part of a local community, to share its concerns and to be open to those who seek help, support and resources.

(v)   A house of the Gospel in which, starting at governor and staff level, there is a deliberate attempt to link the concerns of Christ's Gospel with the life of the school, and to do this in educational terms.

(vi)   A place of revelation and disclosure in which the rigour of learning and the art of acquiring skill are seen as parables of the revelation of God and his continuous involvement in his Creation.

(vii) A foster home of enduring values and relationships, in which the selfless care and unlimited love of the Suffering Servant is the model for the life of the community.

(viii) A beacon signalling the transcendent by the development of awe, mystery and wonder through the curriculum, exemplified in acts of corporate worship including contact with the Christian calendar and sacraments.

(ix)   A place where you can see the wood for the trees, for there are attempts to develop an integrated view of knowledge alongside sensitivity to the interests of others, as well as to cross traditional subject boundaries and carry out integrated projects in learning.

(x)   A creative workshop which facilitates a thorough induction into cultural tradition and skills yet allows pupils to practise initiative, change and new direction as they shape their future.

(*A Future in Partnership*, The National Society 1984; page 71.)

In the 1992 National Society Booklet *Looking for Quality in a Church School* nine areas of Church schools' work were identified as potentially reflecting these understandings:

- The School Mission Statement
- The quality of the general education in the school
- The quality of the religious education in the school
- Collective worship
- Relationships in the school
- The spiritual dimension of the curriculum
- The school's approach to special educational needs
- The school's values
- The integrity of the Christian community within the school.

Governors, headteacher and staff should discuss whether the factors that make for a truly welcoming, reassuring, loving and caring atmosphere are fully applied in their school. Together with the teaching and non-teaching staff the governors have a major responsibility for creating a distinctive ethos. Many of the above characteristics can be found in county schools; but the more of them that are present in a Church school as a result of conscious deliberation, the more apparent will be the specifically Christian nature of the school.

Specifically Christian features are often (though not always) more easily achieved in an aided school than in a controlled school. Nevertheless, the General Synod of the Church of England in July 1985 resolved to call upon foundation governors of controlled schools 'to explore, with their other partners on the governing body, ways in which the Church's role in the school may be more fully and positively implemented' (*Positive Partnership*, The National Society, 1985). At the same time it urged governors of aided schools to ensure that their schools reflected the dual function of Church of England schools: to provide a community/ general service as well as a specifically Christian form of education.

Is there a typical Church school?

There are Church schools serving villages, inner city areas and the suburbs. There are small schools with fewer than thirty on the roll and large schools with over fifteen hundred pupils. So the answer to the question is emphatically "No". Every Church school is different and it is essential that every Church school governing body is able to answer the question "What does it mean to us to be the Church school in this place?" in ways that reflect the local community and its traditions as well as placing the school firmly within the Anglican setting. The response that the school develops to the question should be encapsulated in a clear, short Mission Statement which summarises what the school is aiming to do with and for the children in its care. This should be supplemented by a School Development Plan which lays out how the school plans to set about achieving its aim. Such documents should be developed by the Governors and teachers working together. In a Church school they will reflect the Christian foundation and character of the school. The principles outlined in the Mission Statement will be reflected in every school policy that stems from it.

While the National Society has published a range of material to support Church schools in this work and Diocesan Boards of Education have a key advisory role, it is the governors advised by the headteacher and staff, who must develop their own Mission Statement and policies.

As there are several possible models for a Church school, so there are different ways of witnessing to and engaging in the mission of the Church through the agency of a Church school.

In a pluralist society a Church school may serve a community where the overwhelming majority is of a faith other than Christianity. In such circumstances, governors and teachers will find themselves asking many questions about the role of their school.

There is no simple way for governors of Church schools, together with the staff, to address themselves to (and sometimes agonize over) the task of working out the aims and objectives of their school (that is, the model to which they wish to approximate) given the historical, theological, geographical, social and educational circumstances in which the school is set. It is a challenge however, which, with the guidance available to them, governors should be able to face.

The School and the Local Education Authority

The Church school has a degree of autonomy which is very precious. This can sometimes be misapplied as narrow parochialism, but more often it is seen to represent the needs and rights of the 'local' as opposed to the 'central'. Even so, whilst taking the utmost care to safeguard the interests of the school, the governors and teachers in their dealings with the local authority ought to understand the concerns of the wider scene of which their school is a part.

The Education Reform Act 1988 made provision for schools (county, controlled, aided or special agreement) to opt out of being administered by a LEA and become grant-maintained. These possibilities were further developed in the Education Act 1993, and explanation of and comment on them is given in a separate National Society booklet, *Grant-maintained Status and the Church School*.

4

Meetings of the Governing Body

The Role of the Governor

2 To be a governor of a Church school is a responsibility, an important form of stewardship and a real privilege. Like any other skill, it needs to be learned. It requires diplomatic abilities as well as patience and insight. The governors should be very well informed about their school but at the same time keep a certain objectivity in their relationship with it. They need to have a sound understanding of the role of the teachers and other staff and be aware of their skills. Again, there needs to be real trust in which all sides can recognise one another's skills and roles and share difficulties and achievements.

The principal way in which a governor's contribution to the life of a Church school is focused is through the work of a governors' meeting; therefore it is important to attend these regularly and take a full part in them. It is hoped that all governors, whether they are foundation, representative, or co-opted on to the governing body in a controlled school, will enjoy these meetings and the rest of their work as governors, and that they will feel part of the working partnership which is operating for the good of the school and particularly the education of the children within it.

It would be surprising and indeed regrettable if the meetings of the governing body in a Church school, or indeed of its committees, did not begin and end with prayer. This is important not only in offering the whole of the work of the governing body to God but also in focusing the minds of all present on the tasks they have in front of them. It is one of the ways in which the nature of the school as a Christian community is given tangible expression.

Governors are encouraged to attend training courses or meetings about the conduct of the governing body's business, and it is not the intention of this booklet to duplicate that material. In the following pages, therefore, a number of issues are explored which are likely to come up in the course of the annual work of a governing body in a Church school but which would not arise in quite the same way in a county school.

Officers

The governing body will need to elect a Chairman. Although in Church schools there has been a tradition that this is the incumbent of the parish, it is a matter for the governing body to decide, and it is increasingly common for the chair to be taken by another governor. This is sometimes done in order to free the priest to make a greater contribution to the school in other ways.

Governors will need to elect a Vice-Chairman and Treasurer. This latter post may involve considerable work in aided and special agreement schools if there are major building projects expected. A Clerk to the Governors must also be appointed, to take the minutes and deal with correspondence. This person does not have to be a member of the governing body. In some areas the Clerk may still be provided by the LEA, although such a service will probably be charged against the school's delegated budget. In addition, governors may invite officers from the LEA, or the Diocesan Board of Education to provide advice, and to help them make the best decisions for the school.

Reports

At every meeting governors will receive reports from the school and from any committees that they have established. The most important of these is usually the Headteacher's report; this should give an account of the important events in the life of the school since the last meeting, and may draw attention to any matters on which the Headteacher needs advice or guidance. Governors may also receive items from the LEA, the DFEE or the DBE which they need to discuss. Amongst these will be the annual consideration of whether to apply for grant-maintained status, which is required by law. While these items will sometimes form a significant part of the agenda there will always need to be room for issues raised by the governors themselves. There will also need to be formal opportunities to discuss or decide on school policy as the governors have considerable responsibilities in this area. Particularly important areas for policy in Church schools will be those relating to religious education, collective worship, and relationships with the local and wider Church communities. These policies are the responsibility of the whole governing body and not that of the Chairman or incumbent alone.

All of this gives the impression that governing bodies need to have frequent meetings of great length to enact their business. While it is true that governors are required to meet regularly (at least one meeting each term), much time can be saved by delegating some of the work to committees. Time can also be saved at routine business meetings if the governing body is prepared to hold occasional meetings with a less formal atmosphere, when the focus is on one or two topics which require a detailed preparatory discussion before a policy decision is made.

Committees

Section 116 of the Education Reform Act 1988 provides for, and DES *Circular 7/88* (para. 144) encourages, the establishment of committees by governing bodies and such committees can include non-governors as well as governors. Some governing bodies will wish to take advantage of this to involve a wider range of people in their work.

The School Government Regulations have made it clear that some duties cannot be delegated, but specified functions of the governing body can be delegated to committees, and informal working parties can be asked to undertake work on behalf of the full governing body even in areas where the final decision must be made by the full meeting. Good use of this flexibility will make it possible to find additional help from staff, parents and members of the community and to have well thought-out recommendations for the full governing body to consider. It continues to be the job of the Headteacher to manage the school on behalf of the governing body, but the 1986 and 1988 Education Acts require governors to assume more responsibility than in the past. As a result, it is unlikely that all individual governors will be able to keep abreast of all the areas for which they are responsible and this is a further encouragement for governing bodies to make good use of committees and working parties.

The governing body appoints the members of its committees. In doing this in a Church school the governors will want to take account of the importance of having foundation (Church-nominated) governors on each committee and working party. It would not, however, usually be necessary for the Chairman or the Headteacher to be on every committee. Committees should normally make recommendations to the main governing body, but some may be given executive powers, within the limits provided for under the regulations. Each committee should elect its own chairman if the full governing body has not nominated someone for this role. They should also nominate a convenor to ensure that meetings are well serviced. This post might be taken by any member of the committee, although access to the school office might be a consideration in making the appointment.

Most schools would find it helpful to have the following committees:

i. Curriculum

ii. Pupils: admissions and exclusions

iii. Staffing: appointments/development/grievance/discipline

iv. Finance

v. Premises: Buildings/recreation areas/playing fields/lettings

vi. Parents: Annual parents' meeting/home and school liaison/ evening for new parents.

Each committee needs to be given clear terms of reference by the governing body. It is probably unhelpful to have an LMS committee, as there may be a danger of financial considerations dominating educational needs. If in large schools it is necessary to have a co-ordinating committee, this could be formed from the chairmen or convenors of each of the committees listed above.

Matters affecting pupils and staff can be serious, complicated and arise with little warning. It is important that, as well as the Chairman and the Headteacher, some governors are prepared to deal with such matters. They must understand the relevant procedures and legislation and be ready to be called upon at short notice. Equally, in these areas it will be necessary to ensure that there are some governors who do not have direct involvement in the decision-making about individuals, in order that they can be available to take part in appeals procedures should these be needed.

The Curriculum

3 This section sets out very briefly some of the areas of concern appropriate to governors of schools. It is intended to stimulate thought and discussion, and it concludes with a list of questions which could provide the starting point for items on the agenda of a governing body.

Responsibilities

The governing body has the responsibility of determining the curriculum policy for the school as set out in the Articles of Government of each school. This responsibility, however, has to be worked out within a system which includes such factors as the National Curriculum, the policies of the LEA and, in secondary schools, the requirements of the examination system.

Terminology

As part of this work, it can be helpful from time to time for each governing body to clarify some of the educational terminology that is often so confusing to the non-teacher. What is meant by 'the curriculum', or 'the syllabus'? What is an 'attainment target'? What should be the governors' expectations of a primary, infant, junior, middle or secondary school? Should each governor be prepared to discuss his or her view with others? It is inherent in any partnership that each person understands the terms used and can appreciate their practical application in relation to the classroom.

In the Education Reform Act 1988 the Government introduced the National Curriculum, which with religious education forms the entitlement of every child, and is known as the 'Basic Curriculum'. This is the minimum curriculum which every child should receive in school. The School Curriculum and Assessment Authority (SCAA) is responsible for the publication of the National Curriculum. Governing bodies of every school should ensure that their own curriculum policies reflect the content of the National Curriculum and where appropriate the most recent guidance from their LEA.

The formulation of policy should involve governors directly in two ways:

i)   they should have the opportunity to discuss with the Headteacher and/or staff with specific responsibilities the way in which teaching and learning has been developing. This will not only help governors to be aware of new educational terminology and areas of content but also encourage staff to forge closer links with the governing body. Time must be set aside in governors' meetings for opportunities to discuss curriculum issues or on occasion devote a special meeting to them.

ii)   they should be closely involved in discussion of aims and objectives for their school. These discussions may be stimulated by National Curriculum documents or grow out of guidelines issued by a DBE or a LEA, but the policies must be created out of the governors' own perception of what their school is and should be.

This is an important stage in the review of the curriculum and governors should feel encouraged to share in the development of the partnership between all interested parties.

The Education (Schools) Act 1992 introduced new arrangements for school inspection. These will be an inspection of each school every four years. The inspection will include an examination of current curriculum policies and the extent to which they are being implemented. For this reason alone it is important that Governors ensure that these policies are up to date.

Balance in the Curriculum

This is a vital question for governors because the creation and maintenance of balance in the curriculum is of crucial importance to the education of the pupil. While the impact of the National Curriculum has been welcomed by many, governors should be aware of the way in which concentration on it to the exclusion of other subjects or content alters the balance across the curriculum as a whole. It is the governors' responsibility to ensure that such policy documents as are considered by them reflect and support the best of what is happening in the classroom. The concept of partnership extends here to cover governors, staff and pupils, as a means of ensuring that new curricular policies do not adversely affect the proper balance within each pupil's learning programme. It is important for governors to recognise and make use of the proven professional skill and knowledge of the staff, while not being overawed or afraid to ask relevant questions.

Each school also makes a public statement of its aims by the way in which it presents itself to the local community, to visitors, parents and pupils. As regular but occasional visitors to the school, governors are in a position to notice aspects of school life of which staff may sometimes be unaware, e.g. the warmth of welcome, the way in which pupils and staff speak with each other, the display areas and the approach to punishment/sanctions. Aspects such as these provide signals concerning the ethos and morale of the school. This is some-times referred to as 'the hidden curriculum'. Governors may wish to consider their policy on 'hidden curriculum' issues as part of their programme of curriculum policy review.

In Church schools there is an expectation that religious education will be an area of particular excellence in the curriculum. Governors will wish to explore ways in which this subject can be supported, and to be assured that, whether it is taught as part of an integrated programme or as a separate subject, it is central to the curriculum as a whole.

An important part of the programme to implement recent curricular changes is the School Development Plan. Every governing body should have discussed and approved this plan, when it was first written. They now need to receive reports on its implementation, and to take part in its review.

Sex Education

Under the Education (No 2) Act 1986 and the Education Act 1993 governors have some specific responsibilities in this area of the curriculum. Detailed advice on this topic is provided in another booklet in this series (see list at back of this booklet). Governors needing further advice in the meantime are recommended to consult their Diocesan Director of Education.

A Checklist of Questions for Governors

1   In this school what do governors consider to be the most important aspect of education?

2   Are educational terms (e.g. attainment targets, programmes of study) explained so that all can understand?

3   At governors' meetings, does everyone feel able to ask any questions or have some been inhibited by lack of knowledge or understanding of the education system? What questions would governors really like to ask?

4   Does the school's curricular provision reflect the school's aims and objectives? Do all governors have a copy of these? Have the governors read them? Do governors and staff review them regularly?

5   Is the distinction and interdependence between curriculum, syllabus and timetable clear to governors?

6   What future changes in curricular balance would the governors like to see, if any?

7   How is the curriculum meeting the demands of a pluralist society, or the needs of children with special needs? Does it offer equal opportunities to pupils of both sexes?

8   If our school is a primary school, are the governors aware of the specific responsibilities for aspects of the curriculum that members of staff have? If a secondary school, have the governors discussed with the Head of Department and other staff the work of each department?

9   What special contribution should RE and collective worship make to the overall balance of the curriculum in a Church school? Do the governors have a definite written policy on RE and worship? How – and how often – do they review it?

10   Is the atmosphere of the school welcoming and pleasant? Are governors encouraged to walk around and meet teachers and non-teaching staff?

11   When did the governors last receive a report on the progress towards the full implementation of the School Development Plan?

12   Are there regular opportunities for governors to spend a day in the school, perhaps once a year?

13   Has the governing body explored a few examples of how the school offers a balance of educational activities for its pupils?

14   As Church school governors, are we aware of the way our school fits in with the local educational authority policies? If our school is an aided school, have we invited a member of the diocesan education team and/or an officer of the LEA to talk with us on curriculum policy matters?

Managing the Budget

4 Historically governing bodies of every aided and special agreement school, and many controlled schools, had built up experience of handling finance, through the trust funds for which they have responsibility, and the finances that they use for maintenance and improvement of their buildings. This meant that they were in a good position to undertake with confidence the responsibilities that they were given under Local Management of Schools. Church school governors should take advantage of the training opportunities offered by LEAs in the implementation of LMS schemes, but they will need to bear in mind that in some respects their schools are different.

'Governors' responsibilities' as a phrase now has two meanings in common usage, and if these are muddled there will be significant financial confusion. Local authority LMS trainers seem to use the phrase to mean those items of the budget which are paid by schools out of funds delegated to them by the LEA. These often include some aspects of internal maintenance. The DFEE uses the same phrase to refer to those items of external maintenance and improvement which are the full responsibility of the governors of aided and special agreement schools, for which the DFEE gives grant aid of 85%. It is easy for governing bodies to become confused. Some have sought to pay for internal maintenance with DFEE grants. Some have tried to fund external maintenance entirely from LMS delegated budgets. In both these cases the consequent confusion and chasing of paper work have consumed considerable time and energy.

It is possible to use money in delegated budgets to assist the funding of the governors' 15% contribution to projects that improve the school. However this should be done with care, and it is normally appropriate to consult the DBE before committing delegated budgets to such purposes (see Section 8, The School Building).

Each local authority scheme for LMS is different in detail and therefore it is not possible to provide specific guidance here. Governors of Church schools should approach their Diocesan Director of Education for assistance and advice on these schemes as they apply to Church schools. There is, however, one point that can be made in these pages. It is assumed that a Church school governing body would bring the Christian principles of honesty and straight dealing to their stewardship of their delegated budget, just as they would apply them to any other part of financial management.

Competitive Tendering

A further aspect of the financial arrangements in school needs some attention at this point, and that is the provisions for competitive tendering. Voluntary aided school governing bodies are not included in the Local Government Act of 1988 list of defined authorities and do not have to meet the requirements for competitive tendering. Nevertheless, any activities carried out in aided schools by employees of the LEA must comply, so provision of school meals will be affected. The four activities in which LEAs have to comply with the Act are:–

1. Cleaning of buildings

2. Maintenance of grounds

3. School meals

4. Maintenance of vehicles

There would appear to be three options available to governing bodies of aided schools with regard to these activities.

Governing bodies are strongly recommended to seek the advice of their Diocesan Director of Education on which of the following is best suited to their particular circumstances:.

(i)   accept the LEA's arrangements without adaptation

(ii)   accept the LEA's arrangements with adaptation

(iii)   make their own arrangements.

Some of the considerations relating to the three options are:

(i)   **Accepting the LEA's arrangements without adaptation**

● the LEA would probably be able to negotiate a better price if all schools had the same arrangements (in some LEAs more than 50% of schools are voluntary aided)

● it would be easier to transfer relief staff from one school to another

● the LEA has the administrative ability to look after payroll and personnel matters

● but –

some schools may feel their particular needs are not catered for or that standards of service are insufficiently monitored.

(ii)   **Accepting the LEA's arrangements with adaptation**

- the particular needs of individual schools would be met

- paragraphs 194 and 196 of DES *Circular 7/88* on LMS both state that individual schools may specify the standards they require for their school within an LEA contract

- the LEA would still be able to use the maximum number of schools in its negotiation for the best price, to transfer staff from one school to another and to look after payroll and personnel matters

- but –

  the LEA would need to spend more time in agreeing arrangements.

(iii) **Making own arrangements**

- the particular needs of the school would be met

- the level and quality of management control might be better

- it would be possible to retain existing staff (but governors should bear in mind the consequences of this in terms of their responsibility for administration and management)

- but –
  it might be difficult to obtain relief staff

- it might be difficult for a single school to obtain as good a price as for a large group of schools; the delegated budget would be based on the LEA's price, so the single school might find itself with smaller funds with which to pay higher costs

- where independent contractors are not used, the school would need to have the administrative capacity to look after ongoing payroll and personnel matters, as well as to monitor work being done.

The governors of voluntary aided schools normally employ all staff other than catering and welfare staff. If they choose to join in their LEA's tendering arrangements they will need to reach arrangement with the LEA on the wording of specifications and contracts. Governors are recommended to seek the advice of their Diocesan Directors of Education on this matter.

School Admissions

5 Governors of aided and special agreement schools are in overall control of admissions, subject to the qualifications outlined in Chapter 11 of the DfEE *Guide*. Governors in controlled schools need to be aware of the arrangements for admission to their school which are operated by the LEA.

Capacity

The first stage in the development of a comprehensive arrangement for the admission of pupils to the school is the establishment of the notional capacity of the school. This is done by reference to the regulations produced from time to time by the DfEE on this subject, which take account of the facilities of the school, the needs of the children and the requirements of the National Curriculum. The provisions of the Education Reform Act 1988 which refer to open enrolment have been implemented and governors will need to monitor the way in which they affect their own school. Basically the capacity of the school is defined, and then the school is deemed to have as many vacancies as the difference between its capacity and its present roll. Thus a school with 245 places and 210 pupils on roll on 1 September has 35 places available for the admission of children in the new academic year.

In administering the admission arrangements in their school governors will need to satisfy themselves that the capacity of the school has been correctly assessed, in accordance with the regulations then in force. They will need to review these figures with the LEA each year; this may generally be a formality, unless the school buildings have been altered during the year, or other circumstances have changed.

Policy

The second stage in establishing adequate arrangements for the admission of pupils is to agree a school admissions policy. In order to undertake this effectively, governors should first consider the extent to which their school serves the needs of the local Christian community, by offering Church school education first to the children of Christian parents, or serves the needs of the wider community by giving priority to those children who live nearest to the school. Some governing bodies will seek to provide for an element of both views of a Church school, within the policy that they operate. It is most common to find schools serving the Christian community's domestic needs in areas where there is a wide choice of school available, and the wider community's needs where there is little or no choice of schools, for example in remote villages. Whatever policy the governors adopt they need to be aware that, like every other aspect of the life of the school, it will be saying something about the governors' perception and understanding of the Gospel.

In either case, an admissions policy needs to be clear and such that governors are enabled to decide between the rival claims of two children for admission to the school on the basis of factual evidence. It should also enable parents to estimate their chances of obtaining admission for their child. Since such policies were first required under the Education Act 1980 many schools have not needed to apply them, as there has been an excess of places in all but a few schools. In recent years, however, the number of schools that are over-subscribed has increased, as a result of the removal of excess places and of some growth in the birth rate. In consequence, many schools are now discovering that they have to apply their policy for the first time.

If the governors of a school wish to review their policy (and most governing bodies should do so on a regular basis), they should first seek advice from their Diocesan Director of Education. They need, however, to understand that it is not possible to produce an 'off-the-peg' policy that will be appropriate in their school. Every admissions policy has to be individual. At this point governors will be confronted with one of the most important and often difficult responsibilities of a governing body. By definition, when a school is oversubscribed some parents will inevitably be disappointed; wrestling with the decision as to whom this shall apply, as reflected in and determined by the admissions policy, can be an agonizing experience.

Criteria

Before drawing up admissions criteria governors should acquaint themselves with their trust deed, for this could stipulate a geographical area of benefit – the parish or other area of residence for the benefit of whose people the school came into being. The trust deed is also likely to refer to the kind of religious practices and teaching the school was intended to promote. A too rigid application of this latter point should be avoided, otherwise the trust deed could become a straitjacket which prevents a Church school from responding to the needs of a very different kind of society from the one in existence when the trust deed was written.

An admissions policy is likely to contain statements like:

> Has a least one parent involved in the work and worship of the Church of England.

> or

> Is resident in the village of ————— .

Priority given to the first of these statements produces a policy which serves the Church's domestic needs, priority to the second serves the needs of the wider community. Both the statements above, however, have potential flaws. The first would allow parents to claim places in the school from as far apart as Truro and Durham; some reference to parish or deanery is needed. The second is only clear if the geographic boundaries of the village are clearly established and known to the parents. This discussion will have revealed why it is important for each governing body to tailor their policy to their own needs.

Governors are recommended to consider very carefully the advantages of designing their admissions application form so as to commit parents to apply for a particular class of place in the school rather than for a place in general. Where governors see the role of the school as being one of service to the wider community, as well as to the narrower church-going sector of that community, they might consider dividing available places at the school into so many 'foundation places' which they would fill after taking the Anglican (and perhaps other Christian) connections of the applications into account and so many 'non-foundation places' which they would fill on criteria which take no account of Church connections. The adoption of this practice would deny to an unsuccessful application for a foundation place what might otherwise be a valid ground of appeal based on the success of a non-Church application for a non-foundation place.

The proportion of places available in either category will vary in accordance with the size of the school, the nature of the community and other factors. In some areas extra-district places might constitute a significant group, as might also Christian faith places for the children of the non-Anglican Christian community. The actual number of places available within the non-foundation place category should not be subdivided into so many places for extra district pupils, pupils of other denominations etc. and no quota system should apply. The Commission for Racial Equality considers that an allocation of places to racial or other faith groups in strict numerical terms could be illegal. An admissions policy based on religious grounds is in the Commission's opinion not illegal, provided that when governors fail to admit a pupil that refusal can be justified on religious grounds or on non-racial grounds.

The following are some of the criteria (though the list is by no means exhaustive) which governors may think it right to consider in deciding whether a child would be admitted to their school. They are not given in any recommended order of value and each governing body needs to decide which should apply to its own school.

I General Criteria:

(i)   Has the applicant any brothers or sisters in the school?

(ii) Where does the applicant live in relation to the school and to other schools he/she could attend? (Governors will need to be clear whether they will consider the shortest distance between home and school or the shortest safe route for children and parents to travel from home to school)

(iii) Are there any social or medical reasons why the child should attend the school in preference to another?

(iv) Are there any curricular features at the school which are sought and which are not available at other schools?

(v)   What other reasons may the parent advance for wishing their child to attend the school? Should any of these be acknowledged within the policy?

II Criteria related to Religion:

(i)   Has the child been baptised (and confirmed)?

(ii) Are the parents, and for how long have they been, active worshipping members of an Anglican church? (Governors will need to be clear about their own definition of the words "active worshipping members")

(iii)   Is either parent involved in the work of a local church? (Again "involved in the work of the church" will need definition)

(iv)   In the case of a secondary or middle school, has the child hitherto attended a Church primary school?

(v)   Are the parents active worshipping members of any non-Anglican Christian Church?

(vi)   Do the parents, although worshipping in another faith, wish their child to attend a Church school because of its specifically religious emphasis?

Whatever criteria the governors include in their policy, the order in which they are written is the order in which they must be applied. Therefore, if "at least one parent involved in the work and worship of St ——————'s Church" is placed at the top of the list, all children who meet that criterion must be admitted before any children who do not.

Information for Parents

The Education Act 1980 requires aided and special agreement schools to publish information for prospective parents. The cost of publishing in an agreed format will be met from the school's delegated budget unless the LEA had made other arrangements.

The salient features of the governors' admissions policy will need to be clearly set out, including:

(i)   Target number of admissions

(ii)   Categories of admissions, if any

(iii)   Admissions criteria

(iv)   The arrangements for parents to appeal

The procedure for admissions will need to be clearly explained and an application form in an appropriate format appended.

Application for Places

Parents should be instructed to make application directly to the governors of an aided or special agreement school which they wish their child to attend. In the case of secondary schools it is not suffi-

21

cient to name the school as first choice on an omnibus LEA choice-of-school form.

Each school will need its own form, so constructed as to help the Governors to reach a decision in the light of the criteria laid down in their particular admissions policy.

In the case of secondary schools, governors will need to reach decisions on applications sufficiently in advance of the LEA's decisions about admissions to county and controlled schools that unsuccessful candidates may be allocated places by the LEA in other schools, but this will need careful negotiation with the LEA to avoid the aided schools' being perceived as wishing to 'scoop the pool'. Where applications are made strictly for foundation places governors will need to seek a reference from the appropriate parish clergy in support of the application.

In the case of primary schools, governors will need to reach decisions on applications early enough in the year to all for parents who are disappointed to make an appeal, and then if still not offered a place, to make alternative arrangements for their child. Governors should bear in mind that it is now accepted as good practice for children to be invited to take part in a programme of visiting the reception class before their admission, in order to ensure the smoothest possible transition from home to school.

Interviews

Secondary schools have sometimes set considerable store by the right to interview prospective pupils or their parents and to decide on their applications partly on the basis of the interview. Interviews cannot by their nature be sufficiently objective, and the practice of interviewing could cause governors and headteachers very appreciable difficulty and embarrassment in an appeal committee. It is recommended that this practice should be abandoned if at all possible. This does not preclude the possibility of the governors inviting prospective parents and pupils to view the school before submitting an application.

Points System

It is inevitable that many applications for admission to a given aided secondary school will be so similar that it will be extremely difficult to draw distinctions between them on which decisions can be justified. The adoption of a points system for evaluating applications might in some cases seem to offer a solution. Details of such a scheme should be clear, and all decisions about the number of points to be allocated should be based on objective judgements. The details of the scheme must be made known to intending applications. One disadvantage of such a scheme is that parents may "work the system" in order to increase the points value to their applications. This is, however, also a risk with any admissions policy based on published criteria. Experience of appeals and other case law suggests that governors should not use point systems, unless they are clear and contain no category in which subjective judgements determine the points allocated. Some governors have solved their problems by using distance of travel to school as a means of differentiating between applications that otherwise seem to be of equal weight. If this is done it must be clearly stated on the admissions policy. The method by which the distance is calculated should also be shown.

Parental Undertakings

The question of whether or not prospective parents may be asked for an undertaking not to exercise their legal rights of withdrawal of their child from either religious worship or religious teaching (or both), in the event of their being admitted to the school, is an extremely difficult one which has not yet been tested in the courts. It is, however, quite clear that a child may not be required, as a condition of attending a maintained school (this includes aided schools) to attend any place of worship or to abstain from attending such a place. Parents will have been made aware, in the published information on the school and in the statement of admissions policy, of the religious character of the school, and it is appropriate for governors to ask a question in the following form:

'Do you wish your child to participate in the religious education and worship of the school?'

No undertaking, sought or given, in an admissions policy can affect the parents' legal right to withdraw their children from RE or worship subsequent to their admission to the school. For this reason there may be little real value in asking parents to sign undertakings.

Mid-Course Admission

The admissions policy adopted by the governors must cover the question of admissions to fill casual vacancies arising during the school year as well as normal admissions at the beginning of the year. In general, changes of school tend to hinder rather than advance a child's education, and parents who have been unsuccessful in securing a place for their child at the beginning of the year should not be told that, in the event of a first-year vacancy arising once the school term has started, their application may be reconsidered or that their child will be place on a casual vacancy waiting list.

There will naturally be cases of children having to change schools because the family has moved from one area to another, and applications on behalf of such children for admission in mid-course will need to be treated sympathetically. Vacancies for first-year places may also occur before the beginning of the school year but after the governors have decided upon their admissions list. A policy for dealing with vacancies of this sort will need to form a part of the governors' admissions policy, but the undesirability of keeping alive the hopes of parents for something that may be unlikely to occur should be borne in mind.

The Right of Appeal

When a parent wishes to appeal against the refusal to admit a child to an aided or special agreement school Schedule 2 of the Education Act 1980 as amended by the Education Act 1993 lays down the following three options for the constitution of an appeals committee to be set up by the governing body. The panel may consist of:

(i)   three members, one member will be appointed by the governors, one from a list prepared by the LEA and there will be one lay member.

(ii)   five members, two members will be appointed by the governors, two from the LEA list and one lay member.

(iii)   seven members, three will be appointed by the governors, three from the LEA list and one lay member.

(The governors' appointees may include one or more governors but the Chairman, although a nominee of the governors, may NOT be a governor of the particular school in question. In practice, most governing bodies accept a chairman chosen from a list prepared by the Diocesan Director of Education). The 1993 Act requires the governors to establish a list of lay members of appeals panels. This process must include a public advertisement, which would in practice be shared by several schools.

The 1980 Act lays down basic requirements as to procedure:-

(i)   the appeal must be made in writing, with the grounds being specified;

(ii)   the person(s) submitting the appeal is/are to be given the opportunity of appearing before the committee and making oral representations;

(iii)   the appellant is to be allowed to be accompanied by a friend or be represented by another person;

(iv)   a simple majority of votes cast will decide the appeal, with the Chairman having a second or casting vote;

(v)   the committee's decision is to be conveyed in writing to the person(s) making the appeal;

It is important that governors involved in appeals cases should familiarise themselves with the relevant section of the 1980 Act. This is an area where justice has be done and be seen to be done. This type of appeal committee, together with many others, is under the scrutiny of the Council on Tribunals which has issued details guidance. Appeals committee members are recommended to study the Council's guidance and to liaise closely with their Diocesan Director of Education. The decision of the appeals committee will be binding on the governors.

An appeal hearing will have to consider two distinct issues. Firstly it must consider whether the governing body has correctly administered its published policy. If the panel is convinced that the policy has been correctly administered, the panel then considers whether there might still be space in the school for the appellant's child. At this stage the governors will have to show that their school is already full and that any further admissions would adversely effect the education of the existing pupils. One of the results of an appeal can be that the governors are made aware of those parts of the admissions policy which are insufficiently precise.

Governors, Parents and Teachers

6 The building-up of trust between school and parents is of crucial importance; it requires tact, honesty, a sense of humour and, sometimes, the wisdom of Solomon.

There should develop a willingness on the part of both governors, teachers and parents to acknowledge weakness as well as strength, failure as well as success or ignorance as well as knowledge. Many parents have received as much formal education as teachers, and whilst they may not have all the professional techniques they can be keenly aware of educational theory. Other parents may have experienced failure in their own formal education and therefore may find difficulty in discussing their children's progress with teachers. Symptoms of this previous experience of failure are as likely to be aggression as inhibition. Whatever their background the beliefs, hopes and fears of parents should be treated with respect and sensitivity. Increasingly the school and home must be seen as a partnership.

Maintaining good relationships with parents is not just the responsibility of parent governors, although they do have a major contribution to make in this area. Every member of the governing body should be concerned to ensure that relationships with all the parents in the school are maintained at a good level. The basis of all human relationships in a Church school should be that of Christian love and understanding, and this should be the standard by which relationships with the parents are assessed.

The School Brochure

For many parents, the relationship with the school begins with their first visit when they will meet members of the school staff and receive copies of the school's Information for Parents. This is a document required to be prepared by each school by the Education Act 1980 and it has to include a number of pieces of information about the governing body and its policies. The following items must appear:–

1) The names of all members of the governing body and the address at which the Chairman and Clerk to the Governors can be contacted.

2) The governors' admissions policy, details of how the parents may exercise their right of appeal and any other information which the governors might wish to provide to do with the admission of a child to the school.

3) A summary of the school's curriculum policy, including a statement about the governors' policy on sex education.

4) In secondary schools, the school's result in the previous year's examinations.

It is helpful if, in addition, parents are informed about the way in which the school understands its role in the community as a Church of England or Church in Wales school. This will include something about the governors' policy on school worship, and the way in which religious education is taught in the school. Inevitably, this is quite a long document and governors will be concerned to ensure that the way in which it is presented gives the parent a clear impression of the school. It is part of the way in which governors and the staff show their commitment to good communication and good relationships with parents.

Consulting with parents

Governors will from time to time make decisions on matters about which the parents may have strong opinions. It is important for governors to ensure that they are aware of parents' views on major issues, and it is worthwhile, where important decisions have to be made, to delay them in order to be certain that the parents' views are understood. Where there is an active parents' association or parent-teachers association this may provide a good forum for such discussions to take place. The governors will need to be certain that such groups represent the opinions of the whole parent body. A further means of consultation with parents can be the annual parents' meeting.

The Annual Parents' Meeting

7 The Education (No 2) Act 1986 imposed the requirement that each governing body must hold a meeting for parents at least once in each academic year at which the governors' Annual Report to parents is to be presented and discussed, as are any motions proposed by the parents. The Act and subsequent regulations indicate the minimum range of information that must be provided in the report, the formal machinery by which parents may bring forward motions for debate, and the way in which governors are required to respond to any of these motions which may be passed. Since the Education (Schools) Act 1992 governors have also to report progress on the implementations of action plans following any inspection to this meeting. Similarly, since the Education Act 1993 governors must report any decision arising from their annual consideration of grant-maintained status.

The earliest of these meetings were not well attended, largely due to the unfortunate timing of the implementation of this requirement. Indeed, some schools adopted an approach which complied with the letter of the law but failed to aid and improve the quality of communication between the school and the parents; this hardly helped to boost the attendance. In Church schools it is important that a broader view is taken, and that what is done for, and in the context of, these meetings demonstrates and develops mutual trust and openness. In other words, the annual meeting should be a means of helping to create and sustain the special ethos that a Church school should try to develop.

The Annual Report

The governors' Report should contain an account not only of those things prescribed by law or regulation as outlined in the DFEE *Guide to the Law*, but also of all the activities of the governing body during the previous year which have been important or designed to enhance the life and witness of the school. Governors should usually write the Report themselves and not delegate this task to the Headteacher or their Clerk, so that they present the work that they have done in the way in which they wish it to be communicated.

The Report should, of course, be presented in a style that will help the parents to assimilate the information that it contains. Where parents of children at the school speak a language other than English as their first language, the governors should seek the assistance of the LEA in translating the report into the first language of these parents. Special means of communication will need to be considered if it is known that some of the parents are not literate in their own first language.

Governors should also make available details of the financial support that they have received from the parish and the diocese, not only because these are donations of money, and therefore covered in the regulations, but also because it is important for the parents to know that the school receives this support if they are invited to contribute to the governors' liability for improvements and maintenance.

Preparing for the meeting

Good preparation and planning will help to ensure that the meeting makes a positive contribution to the life of the school. In setting the date, time and place for the meeting, the governors should consider whether their decisions are likely to make the meeting more or less attractive to parents. In particular, the context of the meeting, the other activities that are arranged for the evening, and the type of refreshment offered may all need to be discussed. The atmosphere should be welcoming and, as far as possible, within the constraints of the school, the physical conditions should be comfortable. Governors should decide in advance how the room will be arranged, and how parents will be welcomed. If the formal proceedings are to begin with prayers (as is appropriate in a Church school), these will also need preparation.

Governors should know before the meeting how issues associated with eligibility to vote are to be resolved and the level of attendance necessary for resolutions to be put to the vote. They should have planned the agenda for the evening, including who will chair the meeting, and who will present the Annual Report. It may well be that, where governors have taken responsibility for writing different parts of the Report, those who have written a particular section should present that section to the meeting. This will demonstrate to the parents how the governors organise their work and share the respon-sibilities that they hold. Where the governors are aware that there is concern among the parents about an aspect of the life of the school they should ensure that the discussion on these topics is open and well organised, so that parental concerns are aired in a way which is constructive. As these include the conduct of individual members of staff, the governors should ensure that, at the beginning of the meeting, a clear statement is made from the chair about the limits which will be imposed on such personal discussions. This is particularly important in the context of aided school governors' responsibilities as employers.

Formal motions

Where there are sufficient parents present the meeting can consider and vote on formal motions. These may require a response from the governors, the LEA or the Headteacher. It is important that parents understand the process that these motions stimulate. The legal requirement is that, following the passing of a motion at a parents' meeting, the governors must decide to whom the motion should be addressed, and consider it themselves if appropriate.

Conduct of the meeting

In general terms, these meetings should be conducted in a spirit of openness and frankness. Clearly there are some areas of the governors' work, principally to do with matters concerning individual staff or children, which must not be discussed, but usually most of the work of the governors can be considered. Questions should, wherever possible, be answered fully. Most parents will be encouraged by such an approach to continue to put their trust in the governors. Conversely, answers which are seen to be incomplete or evasive only create distrust and suspicion. Governors should err on the side of providing more information than has been requested rather than less. Whilst time should be provided to enable all the issues which the parents wish to raise to be dealt with, it is useful if the governors have previously published a time schedule within which parents know that meeting will be conducted. This is particularly important where parents have to arrange for the care of their children while they attend the meeting.

After the meeting

As soon as possible after the meeting, governors should discuss the events of the evening and in particular how they will respond to any issues that were raised or motions that were passed. They will need to decide which of these matters it is their own responsibility to deal with and which should be referred to the Headteacher or the LEA. If questions have been raised that it has not been possible to answer completely on the night, a full response should be prepared and circulated to all parents as quickly as possible. While the legal requirements is that action following the motions passed by the parents at an Annual Meeting must be reported to the next one, most governing bodies will wish to ensure that parents are aware of the decisions that have been taken as soon as possible.

Summary

The Annual Parents' Meeting has the potential to provide an additional means of communication between the school and the parents of pupils. As parents become used to the idea that these meetings are now a normal part of the life of a school, and attendance is a normal part of the responsibility of being a parent of a school-age child, then it must be expected that attendances will improve and that the meetings will become progressively more useful. In many parts of the country this is already happening. Within Church schools governors will wish to conduct such meetings in ways which reflect the Christian foundation of the school, enhance the quality of its communications, and develop the partnership between school and parents which is an essential part of the successful education of the children.

The School Building

8 Almost all Church school buildings are owned by a trust, and the Trustees are usually either people connected with the local church or a diocesan organisation. In all Church schools, the governors should take careful note of the state of the buildings and ensure that action is taken to keep them in good repair and to see when improvements are needed.

Funding

Internal maintenance of the building will be for the governors to undertake, using the budget delegated to them by the LEA. In controlled schools, the same will apply to the external maintenance of the school, if this area has been delegated to schools under the LEA scheme. In aided and special agreement schools, external maintenance is the responsibility of the governors; they have to contribute 15% of the cost of this from their own funds, or funds which they raise and the DfEE pays a grant of 85% of the total cost. Naturally the DfEE has rules about the amount of money which governors are allowed to spend on its behalf without obtaining prior approval. Before the governors of any school initiate a project they should ensure that they are aware of the rules that exist at that time, and have got the necessary approval. The Diocesan Director of Education, or a member of the staff of the DBE, should be able to provide help and guidance with this.

Developing a building

Where governors, in consultation with the Headteacher and the staff of the school, feel that some improvement is needed to the building, they should consult both the LEA and the DBE about their plans. In controlled schools the funding for such projects will need to come from the LEA. In aided and special agreement schools, funding will be on the same basis as for maintenance of buildings, but the rules about obtaining grants from the DFE are somewhat tighter and the DBE will be able to provide guidance on this. For major projects the governors may be able to look to the DBE for assistance, particularly with the payment of contractors, as this has to be done before grant is claimed from the DfEE.

In most schools there will be a number of projects that governors would like to see undertaken. These may range from the provision of a sink in a classroom to a complete re-modelling of the internal space. Occasionally the favoured solution may be to build a new school on a new site. While it will not be possible to do everything at once, it is important to make a list of desired projects and then to develop a plan for achieving them. Such planning will need to be related to the school development plan.

It is also helpful if governing bodies identify a programme of mainte- nance which can be carried out regularly, to put alongside the development programme. Progress towards achieving this should be monitored from time to time. Such programmes are important in enabling governors to plan their budgets, using either their own funds or funds delegated to them from the LEA.

Health and Safety

A particular concern of all governors is the health and safety of all those using the building. A group of the governors should arrange to inspect the building with these issues in mind on a regular basis, prob- ably accompanied by the Health and Safety Representative of the staff, in order to identify any action which needs to be taken. It is important that any work is identified and put in hand promptly, and that this group takes account of the need for safe working practices so that everyone can use the building in safety.

Maintenance

While it is clear that maintenance has to be planned, and kept within a budget, nevertheless it is important that necessary maintenance is not delayed. Delays in maintenance usually result in deterioration of the building, which may be unsightly, and thus deter parents from placing their child in the school in the short term, and also lead to higher costs in the long term. This is particularly true of re-decora- tion, which can often be the lowest priority. The morale of staff and children is affected by the environment in which they work and it is generally accepted that levels of internal vandalism are related to chil- dren's and young people's perception of their environment.

Development

Many school governing bodies are now considering the production of a School Building Development Plan to put alongside the School Development Plan. This would help in the planning of both maintenance and a programme of school improvement, to provide for the needs of the children and staff and to meet the growing demands of the Basic Curriculum.

The School and the Local Church

9 The Church school, like the Church, should be concerned to serve the community and to do this with sensitivity and compassion. The school is not the place for narrow evangelism (the children are a captive audience) but the teachers should be aware of their responsibility to witness to the truths and values of the school's Christian foundation. This is an immensely tender area and should be approached with humility and care. It is probably the case, however, that children are far more resilient in these matters than their parents and have an instinctive feel for what makes sense and what does not.

The school itself should feature regularly on the agenda of the parochial church council and should be seen to be part of the life of the Christian community of that place. How this is worked out in practice will depend upon local factors.

All Church schools should maintain good relationships with the worshipping community at the local church. The governors nominated by the parish church have an important communication role here, but, in the same way that is not just the parent governors' job to maintain good relationship with the parents, neither is it just the Church governors' job to maintain good relationships with the church. For most schools this relationship will focus principally on the church in whose parish the school operates. But, for some, the relationship will be broader than this because the school serves a number of parishes or may, in the case of secondary schools, have its principal ties with the whole Deanery. All Church schools should, however, maintain a close working relationship with the Diocesan Board of Education. In many cases this will be given practical expression by nomination to the governing body of representatives from the Diocese. Most Church schools will also want to express their involvement with the Church nationally. This can be achieved through membership of the National Society, which helped to found nearly every Church school in England and Wales and still provides support and resources today (see page 42 for further information). Where there are churches of other denominations in the area served by the school the governors will wish to ensure that there is a well-developed relationship with this group. Indeed, for some schools this will spread to groups from other faiths as well.

There will, however, usually be a small number of churches, often only one, with which the school is in a special relationship. This is expressed by involvement of the church (not just the parish clergy) in the work of the school, and the school (not just the Headteacher) in the life of the church. The governors' policy on worship in the school will take account of the tradition of the local church as well as the Anglican Church at large, and there should be elements in common between the worship of the school and that of the parish church. This does not mean that they will always be the same. The school will wish to use much material which is particularly appropriate to the age and maturity of the children. The church must provide worship which is appropriate to the adult congregation, as well as to its members who are younger.

But it is not just in worship that Church and school should meet. The lives of the two communities should be so interwoven that there is never an opportunity for people at the school to feel neglected, nor for members of the church to feel ignorant about the school.

The School and the Parish Clergy

The roles of the parish priest in the Church school are those of pastor, friend and theologian. He or she should hold the school in prayer and keep it in the mind of the church. The priest need not necessarily teach, but should be able to offer the school love, refreshment and concern for all its members. The role is both reflective, in that the priest should be able to think about the school in the light of a theological and spiritual understanding, and affirmative, in that the priest should be able to remind its members of their worth in the sight of God.

As Geoffrey Duncan observes in *Faith for the Future* (edited by Graham Leonard and Joanna Yates, The National Society/Church House Publishing, 1986), 'one of the features of Church school governing bodies is the ex-officio status as a governor of the incumbent (the 'principal officiating minister', to use the legal term)". Furthermore, it still tends to be the tradition with a small but increasing number of exceptions that the incumbent becomes chairman of the governing body. Where this near-automatic relationship works well, it is a great and obvious benefit of the school. Where it does not work well the effect on the school, equally obviously, can be disastrous.

Where training is provided parish clergy should avail themselves of it, to help them to perform well as governors and potential chairmen; where it is not available they should press the DBE for action in this regard. They should be under no illusion about the increasing importance and complexity of the role of chairman of governors.

Under both education and charity law the governing bodies of aided schools have certain autonomous powers. They should, however, always be mindful that the way they exercise their autonomy can have an effect on the impact of the Church as a whole on the national educational scene. It is important that governing bodies, as members of an episcopal Church, have regard to any relevant diocesan policy (indeed, this is in effect required of them by the Diocesan Boards of Education Measure 1991), and as members of a national Church they should also bear in mind General Synod and National Society policies. If their school is in union with the National Society they should also observe the terms of that union.

The foundation governors, serving both school and Church, have a dual role to play: they represent the one to the other and should bring their Christian insight and understanding to bear upon both.

School Inspection

10 The Education (Schools) Act 1992 introduced a new pattern of inspection for schools in England and Wales. Details of the ways in which this Act affects Church schools have been fully described in other National Society publications (see the list on page 40). The governors have a key role in the inspection process, both in approving and supporting school policy documents and in preparing and implementing the Action Plan following an inspection.

All governors should be aware of the special arrangements for the inspection of those aspects of the school that are conducted in accordance with the school trust deed. They should also be aware that the National Society has provided a national training and registration scheme for those people who wish to offer themselves as inspectors of church schools. The Society has also published a Handbook for the Inspection of Church schools and every Anglican school should be aware of its contents.

As well as their formal responsibilities the governors should also be aware of the impact on the morale of staff that this new process of inspection can have. An important role for some governors during the inspection process may be to ensure that the staff are encouraged and supported.

Appointing Staff in Church Schools

This subject is covered very fully in the National Society's publication *Church School Staffing* (Lois MR Louden and David S Urwin, The National Society/Culham College Institute/ Southwark DBE, 1995). Every governor will need to be clear on the extent to which it is important to ensure that a practising christian is appointed to this particular post. This is clearly essential for senior staff, but does such a requirement apply to the school secretary or a dinner supervisor? All staff will need to receive a programme of induction into the school which will include developing their understanding of what it means to undertake their duties in a Church school. All these issues are explored fully in the publication mentioned at the beginning of this paragraph.

Conclusion

The School Community – The Ideal and the Reality

11 There is no point in pretending that a school is ideal if it is not, and the chances of any school being absolutely ideal are nil. We have to live and work with reality. We are up against all kinds of pressures, however:

- from within the school, there is the natural wish to believe that all is well and deny that anything can be wrong;

- from the outside, the school may be regarded as a scapegoat, the cause of all society's ills;

- from the Church itself may come the accusation that the school is not serving the Church sufficiently.

Pessimistic feelings need to be balanced by the good and marvellous things that can also happen; by the awareness of parents, and by the appreciation they show, of what the school is attempting and achieving; by the generosity of spirit and care shown by many clergy; – but above all by those astonishing and moving moments when a child suddenly 'sees'.

Christianity and the School

Our school communities, after all is said and done, are mixtures of good and bad. Christian schools are no exception – but they, of all schools, should have the resources and the insight to face the situation squarely. If the Christian faith has nothing to say or do in this setting it ought to be abandoned. But if it has insights, if it has real clues about the nature of human behaviour and the meaning of life, it ought to be making itself known. This will be achieved by struggling with the problems together, and celebrating the good and positive aspects of community life.

Governing Church schools involves a considerable commitment of time and energy. It is not necessary for every governor to be an expert teacher, lawyer or accountant, but it is important that they are each able to make their own contribution to the life of the school.

Willingness to listen and to share good common sense and an experience of life are characteristics which all schools will value highly in their governors.

Governors of Church schools carry a heavy responsibility, but where they have good relationships with staff, pupils and parents, as well as support from the LEA, DBE and National Society, they can find their work more and more rewarding.

A Selection of National Society Publications

Available by mail order from the National Society at the address on page 42:

Church School Inspection: A Guide for Schools of the Church of England and the Church in Wales by Lois M R Louden and David S Urwin. A practical training guide produced as a companion to *Mission, Management and Appraisal,* by the same authors. (NS £15.00)

Inspection Handbook for Section 13 Inspectors in schools of the Church of England and the Church in Wales by Alan Brown and David W Lankshear. (NS £15.00) A handbook to the whole process of inspection under Section 13 of the Education (Schools) Act 1992.

Open The Door: Guidelines for worship and for the inspection of worship in voluntary and grant-maintained Church schools by David Barton, Alan Brown and Erica Brown (NS/Oxford Diocesan Education Services, £3.00).

Church School Staffing by Lois M R Louden and David S Urwin. An essential resource for the whole process of selecting and appointing teachers, headteachers and support staff in Church schools of all kinds: aided, controlled and grant-maintained. (NS £15.00)

Available by mail order post free from the National Society (new titles issued FREE to members on publication):

School Worship (NS £1.50). For teachers and governors in Church and country schools.

The Curriculum: A Christian View (NS £1.50). A discussion of the values on which the curriculum should be based.

Primary School Worship by Alan and Eric Brown (NS £3.00). A practical guide for county, voluntary, grant-maintained and independent schools.

Opening Their Eyes: Worship and RE with Children with Special Needs by Erica Musty (Brown) (NS £1.50). Guidance for teachers in schools of all kinds.

Mixed Blessings: The Special Child in Your School by Erica Brown (NS £3.00). Advice and information for mainstream schools facing the challenges of pupils with special educational needs.

Looking for Quality in a Church School by David W Lankshear (NS £2.00). An introduction to appraisal and school inspection.

Sex Education: Guidelines for Church School Governors by Alan Brown (NS £2.00). Questions for discussion and curriculum guidelines for a potentially delicate subject.

Preparing for Inspection in a Church School by David W Lankshear (NS £2.50). Essential reading for governors, headteachers and teachers now that the new system for the inspection of maintained schools has come into operation.

Continuing in the Way: Children, Young People and the Church by Leslie J Francis and David W Lankshear (NS £1.75). A survey with important implications for the Church in the Decade of Evangelism.

In the Catholic Way (NS/The Church Union £3.00) and *In the Evangelical Way* (NS £3.00). The results of further analysis of Anglican parishes of different traditions and their contact with young people.

Small Schools by David W Lankshear (NS £3.00). An up-to-date guide for all concerned with small schools and their roles in the community.

Christianity in the Agreed Syllabus by Alan Brown (NS £2.50). An authoritative and helpful guide to RE in schools.

The Multi-Faith Church School by Alan Brown (NS £2.25). Not a contradiction in terms, but a common and encouraging reality.

Moral Education by Janina Ainsworth and Alan Brown (NS £3.00). A topical and helpful guide for both Church and county schools.

For details of application froms for teaching posts, staff contract forms, books for school and parish education and all the services provided by the National Society, please send for a free catalogue from the address on page 42.

THE NATIONAL SOCIETY

The National Society (Church of England) for Promoting Religious Education supports everyone involved in Christian education – teachers, school governors, students, parents, clergy, parish and diocesan education teams – with the resources of its RE centres, courses, conferences and archives.

Founded in 1811, the Society was chiefly responsible for setting up the nationwide network of Church schools in England and Wales, and still helps them with legal and administrative advice for head-teachers and governors. It was also a pioneer in teacher education through the Church colleges. The Society now provides resources for those responsible for RE and worship in any school, lecturers and students in colleges, and clergy and lay people in parish education. It publishes a wide range of books and booklets and two magazines, *Crosscurrent* (free to members) and *Together with Children*.

The National Society is a voluntary body which works in partnership with the Church of England General Synod Board of Education and the Division for Education of the Church of Wales. An Anglican society, it also operates ecumenically, and helps to promote inter-faith education and dialogue through its RE centres.

For a free resources catalogue and details of individual, corporate and associate membership contact:

> The Promotions Officer
> The National Society
> Church House
> Great Smith Street
> London SW1P 3NZ
> Telephone: 0171-222 1672
> Fax: 0171-233 2592